THE USBORNE YOUNG SCIENTIST
CARS

Contents

4   Early motorcars
6   Understanding cars
8   Classic cars
10   Sports racers
12   Grand Prix racing
14   Learning to race
16   At the race track
17   Rally cars

18   Dragsters
20   Weird wheels
22   Car design
24   Car production
26   Green cars
28   The world land speed record
30   Record breakers
32   Index/Going further

Credits

Written by Jonathan Rutland and Margaret Stephens
Art and editorial direction David Jefferis
Editorial revision Margaret Stephens
Text Editor Eliot Humberstone
Design Iain Ashman
Design revision Robert Walster
Technical consultant Roger Ames
Illustrators Malcolm English, Terry Hadler, John
Hutchinson, Frank Kennard, Jack Pelling, Michael
Roffe, Robert Walster, Sean Wilkinson, Hans Wiborg-
Jenssen, John Scorey and Chris Lyon.

Acknowledgements

We wish to thank the following individuals and
organizations for their assistance.

John Barker
Performance Car
Car Magazine
BMW (GB) Ltd
General Motors Ltd
Mercedes-Benz Ltd
Brands Hatch Racing Ltd
Citroën UK Ltd
Porsche Cars GB Ltd
Project Thrust

Usborne Publishing Ltd
Usborne House
83-85 Saffron Hill
London EC1N 8RT

Printed in Belgium

This edition published 1991
Based on the Young Engineers Book of Supercars,
published 1978.

The name Usborne and the device ⛴ are trademarks
of Usborne Publishing Ltd.

Introduction

If you compare the sleek lines and speed of the latest Formula 1 racer with the clumsy design and spluttering performance of the first steam carriage, it is amazing that one grew out of the other. But that is exactly what happened.

From the first motorcars that crept along at a snail's pace puffing steam, to the development of the petrol engine and the latest top-speed dragster, the history of the car is fascinating and exciting.

In this book, you will find out about how a car works, learning to race, sportscars, the latest robot technology in car factories and what happens at the Formula 1 race track. You will also discover the world of dragsters and rally cars.

Everything is explained simply and there are experiments to show you the principles behind car engineering. You can even have a go at designing your own car.

This picture gives you a look at the parts which make up a modern rally car, the Lancia Integrale. Rally cars are always ordinary production cars, although with many changes and modifications.

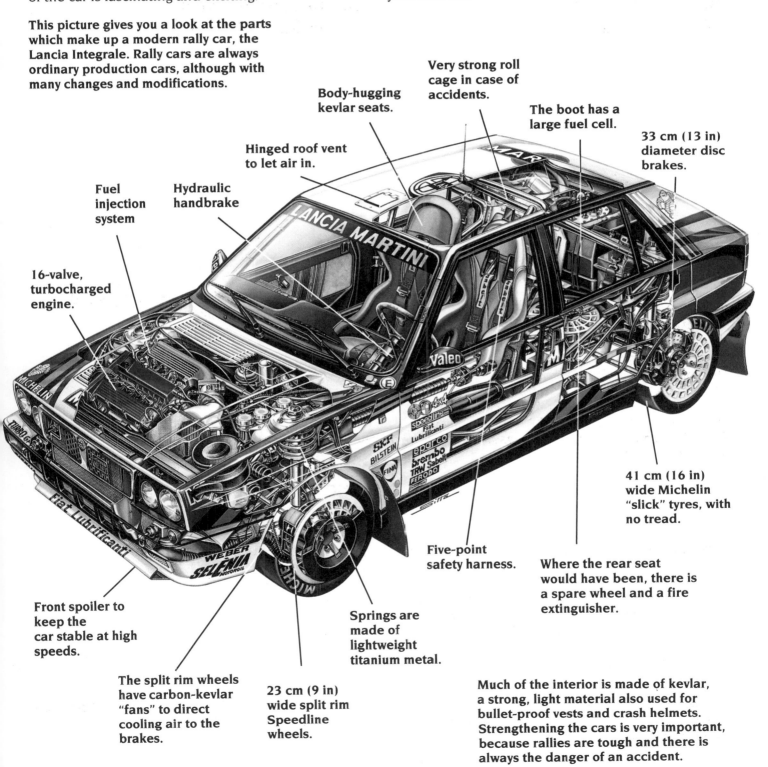

Very strong roll cage in case of accidents.

Body-hugging kevlar seats.

The boot has a large fuel cell.

33 cm (13 in) diameter disc brakes.

Hinged roof vent to let air in.

Fuel injection system

Hydraulic handbrake

16-valve, turbocharged engine.

41 cm (16 in) wide Michelin "slick" tyres, with no tread.

Five-point safety harness.

Where the rear seat would have been, there is a spare wheel and a fire extinguisher.

Front spoiler to keep the car stable at high speeds.

Springs are made of lightweight titanium metal.

The split rim wheels have carbon-kevlar "fans" to direct cooling air to the brakes.

23 cm (9 in) wide split rim Speedline wheels.

Much of the interior is made of kevlar, a strong, light material also used for bullet-proof vests and crash helmets. Strengthening the cars is very important, because rallies are tough and there is always the danger of an accident.

Early motorcars

The earliest ancestor of the motorcar was built in the 18th century by a French engineer, Nicholas Cugnot. His first vehicle, shown on the right, was steam powered and not very successful.

In the 19th century, engineers tried to improve the design of these steam carriages, which were too slow and cumbersome to achieve widespread use. Then in 1885, there came a major breakthrough when Karl Benz, a German engineer, made the first vehicle powered by a petrol engine. This was the start of a revolution and soon petrol-powered vehicles were to replace horse-drawn vehicles and rule the road.

Cugnot's steam carriage of 1770 had a tank mounted at the front to boil water in. The steam power generated by the boiling water turned the vehicle's front wheel through a system of piston, cylinder, rods and cranks. It was designed to haul cannon for the French army, but proved of very little use. Top speed was 5 km/h (3 mph) and every 15 minutes it had to stop to build up steam again. The heavy tank made it hard to steer and Cugnot's first carriage crashed. He did make another, but by then the army had sensibly lost all interest.

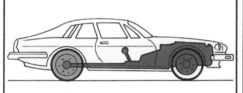

Front engine, rear wheel drive.

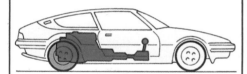

Mid engine, rear wheel drive.

Rear engine, rear wheel drive.

Front engine, front wheel drive.

These diagrams show some of the different ways in which engines and driving wheels can be arranged. From top to bottom, the cars are: a Jaguar XJ-S, a Matra Bagheera, a Porsche 911 and an Alfa Romeo Alfasud. Front engine with front wheel drive is the most common design in modern cars.

This is a Renault leading the field in the first Grand Prix race, held in 1906 near Le Mans in France. The Renault completed the 1,238 km (769 mile) course at an average speed of 101 km/h (63 mph). Previous big events had been raced on public roads, but were banned as too dangerous. This was why closed circuit races like the Grands Prix were started.

4   In 1902, the French government tried to make motorists use alcohol fuel manufactured from potatoes.

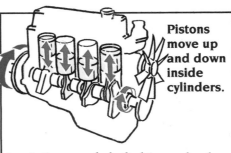

Pistons move up and down inside cylinders.

A rotating crankshaft drives wheels through a gearbox and driveshaft.

This picture shows the first car to run successfully with a petrol engine. It was built by Karl Benz in 1885. To the right is a diagram of a typical modern engine, based on the Benz principles. Petrol vapour is ignited at the top of each cylinder by an electric spark plug. The

explosions force down pistons which are inside the cylinders. The "up and down" movement of the pistons turns a rod and then a crankshaft, which provides turning power for the wheels. The pistons move one after the other in sequence to provide a smooth flow of turning power.

This 1891 Panhard Levassor had the layout used by many cars ever since. The engine was at the front under the bonnet. The car had a gearbox, foot-operated clutch, rear wheel drive and a radiator to cool the water. The basic principles have been the same for a hundred years.

The Ford Model T was the first car to be made on an assembly line. Before 1908, all cars had been hand made and were very expensive. Mass production techniques meant the time - and the cost - of car making could be drastically reduced.

As the car's popularity grew, so did the number of makes. Soon there were over 500 in the USA alone. The three badges shown above represent makes of cars that all became part of the American General Motors, now one of the world's biggest car makers.

This was the ancestor of all high-performance sports cars. It was called the Skiff because of its boat-like appearance and was built in 1911 for the racing driver René de Knyff by Panhard Levassor. The Skiff's body was a revolutionary step

away from the solid, heavy coachwork of earlier cars. It was built to weigh as little as possible and had the lightweight construction of aeroplanes of that time. Spoked wheels were also used to reduce the weight of the car.

In 1896, Henry Ford's first car was the only car in Detroit. He had to chain it up when he left it unattended.

Understanding cars

The key to understanding how cars work is knowing that they are made up of seven systems. These are engine, transmission, body, steering, brakes, electrics and suspension - all shown on these pages.

The large picture is a skeleton view of a 1930 Bentley racing car. Compare this car with the modern cars pictured around it.

This is a side view of the 217 km/h (135 mph) Bentley.

Early cars had front wheels mounted on a single axle, linked to the chassis by springs.

Early cars had oil or gas lamps, which did not give out much light. Electric ones like this date from 1913 and are much more powerful.

The tyres are air-filled (pneumatic). The first cars had solid tyres. These gave a hard bouncy ride and poor grip, reducing cornering and braking power.

Engine

This is the power-house of the car. It is controlled by a floor-mounted accelerator pedal.

This handbrake, typical of the period, was mounted on the outside of the car. All cars now have handbrakes inside, usually between the front seats.

Transmission

Transmission links the engine to the driving wheels by clutch, gearbox, and differential.

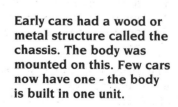

Propeller shaft

Early cars had a wood or metal structure called the chassis. The body was mounted on this. Few cars now have one - the body is built in one unit.

The capacity of the engine is measured in litres or cubic inches, depending on the country. The size refers to the total volume of all the cylinders.

Steering

A rack and pinion steering system turns the wheels left or right. This is controlled by a steering wheel.

Brakes

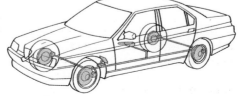

Usually a floor-mounted pedal controls the brakes on all wheels. A hand brake is used for parking.

Electrics

The alternator supplies all the electricity when the engine is running and charges the battery.

A saloon can be made from nearly 60 materials, including steel, aluminium, rubber, plastic and leather.

Body

In almost all modern cars, the body is made of welded pressed steel units.

The large fuel tank carries petrol, which is fed along pipes to the engine by an electric pump. For safety, modern tanks are placed in less exposed positions.

The differential unit is joined to the engine by a propeller shaft. The differential sends variable power to the two driving wheels. Most modern cars do not have a propeller shaft because they are front engine with front wheel drive.

Suspension

Springs and shock absorbers soak up road bumps, allowing a smooth comfortable ride.

Why a differential is necessary

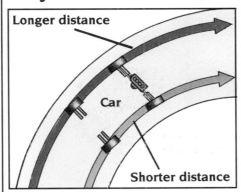

Longer distance

Car

Shorter distance

The differential is an essential component of a car. As a car travels around a bend, the inside wheels cover a shorter distance than the outside wheels. The differential adjusts the power to each driving wheel to cope with this situation.

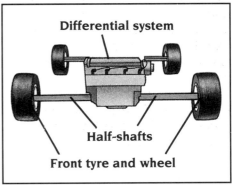

Differential system

Half-shafts

Front tyre and wheel

The driving wheels are attached to an axle split into two halves, called half-shafts. The differential, which is a gear system, lies in the middle. This allows the wheels to run at different speeds.

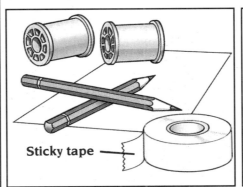

Sticky tape

You can see why a differential is necessary from this experiment. You need two pencils (or two ball point pens), a roll of clear sticky tape, two cotton reels and some paper. If you cannot get cotton reels, try plastic bottle tops.

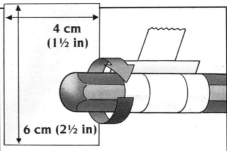

4 cm (1½ in)

6 cm (2½ in)

The pencil should be free to turn inside the sleeve.

Take a piece of paper and cut a shape 4 cm (1½ in) wide and 6 cm (2½ in) long. Wrap it round a pencil and fasten with tape. Make sure the tape does not touch the pencil. The pencil should be able to slide freely in its paper "sleeve".

Tape a coloured dot to each pencil.

Cut two pieces of paper into a square, 1 cm (½ in) by 1 cm (½ in). Colour a dot on each and tape them to the pencils. Now jam the tips of both pencils firmly into the cotton reels, and slip the ends into the paper sleeve.

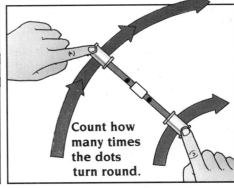

Count how many times the dots turn round.

Rotate your pencil and cotton reel assembly around a sharp bend. Count how many times the dot on the outer pencil turns. Count how many times the dot on the inner pencil turns. The outer dot should turn three times as much as the inner one.

In six years, an average car travels nearly 97,000 km (60, 276 miles). Each wheel will have turned 54 million times.

Classic cars

Motoring began as a noisy, uncomfortable and often messy adventure. But before long engineers began designing cars that gave a smoother ride and were more reliable.

In 1906, Rolls-Royce brought out the Silver Ghost which was the first of this new generation of cars. Other makers, like Mercedes-Benz and Jaguar, soon followed their example by producing cars with comfort, style, performance and reliability.

Many of these cars are now famous classics, and greatly sought after by collectors. Here we have chosen a selection of our own favourite classic cars.

▲ Duesenberg SJ, 1932. Supercharged 6.9 litre engine, top speed 208 km/h (129 mph). By 1937, when the Duesenberg company had collapsed, just 470 SJs had been made.

▲ Rolls-Royce Silver Ghost, 1906. 7 litre engine, top speed about 125 km/h (78 mph). To show its superior quality, the first Silver Ghost was driven day and night for 24,120 km (14,988 miles). It had to make only one repair stop.

▲ Mercedes-Benz Model S, 1927. 6.8 litre engine, top speed 160 km/h (99 mph). This sports car was faster than Mercedes' Grand Prix racing cars of the time, and proved almost unbeatable on the track. It had good brakes, steering and roadholding.

Jaguar XK 120, 1948. 3.4 litre ▶ engine, top speed 212 km/h (132 mph). The first streamlined, high-performance sports car, it won race after race. It was also popular as a road car and fairly cheap to buy. Its engine design is still in use today.

To comply with different countries' various regulations, a Rolls-Royce has to pass more than 204 separate tests.

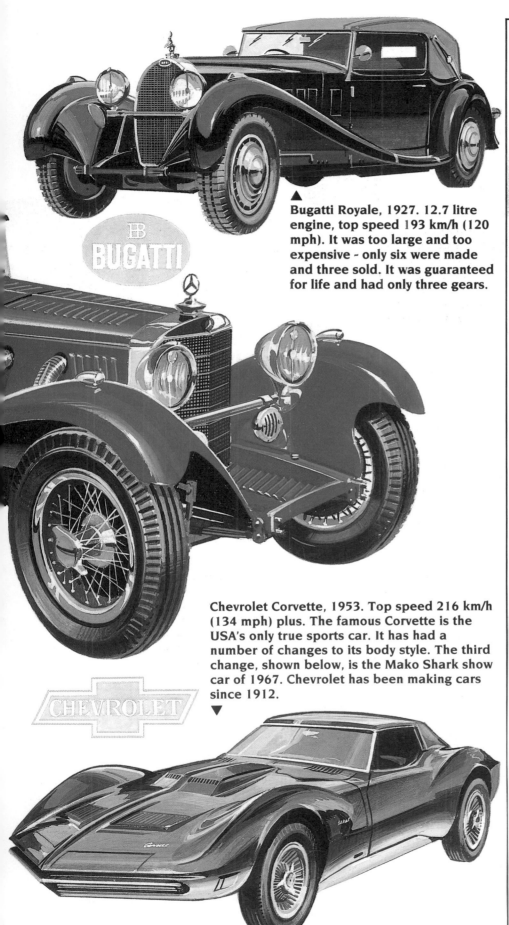

▲ Bugatti Royale, 1927. 12.7 litre engine, top speed 193 km/h (120 mph). It was too large and too expensive - only six were made and three sold. It was guaranteed for life and had only three gears.

Chevrolet Corvette, 1953. Top speed 216 km/h (134 mph) plus. The famous Corvette is the USA's only true sports car. It has had a number of changes to its body style. The third change, shown below, is the Mako Shark show car of 1967. Chevrolet has been making cars since 1912. ▼

Classic cars revived

The Vicarage E-Type

Cars with the styling of famous classics from the past are a money-spinning part of the car-making business. This means that some classics you see on the road may be younger than they look. The Bugatti Royale, shown on the left, is a model that has been revived.

Vicarage Motorcars in the UK are specialists in creating almost brand new versions of classic Jaguars, including the Jaguar Mk ll and the most famous sports car of all time, the E-Type roadster.

The original E-Type was first produced in 1961, and designed by Malcolm Sayer, the engineer behind the Le Mans winning D-Type of the 1950s. Out of production now for many years, the E-Type has been revived by Vicarage with many new improvements. Girling brakes have been added and the steering and suspension have been improved. More supportive seats and a power hood are other modern additions. The car still has the famous E-Type body design, luxurious leather seats and a walnut dashboard.

How do Vicarage make a 30-year old car look brand new? First they take old Jaguar bodies and strip them to their bare metal. Then they shot-blast them for up to 48 hours to make sure the body is free of corrosion. Later, 17 to 24 coats of primer, undercoat, top coat and lacquer are applied to the bodywork. Then it takes two days to hand polish the painted body work. Every mechanical and electrical component is either made new or restored.

At Rolls-Royce a machine called IRMA "squirms" a million times to check that seats will not collapse.

Sports racers

Sports racers compete in the Sportscar World Championship. Famous car manufacturers, such as Jaguar, Porsche, Mercedes and Mazda, know that top performances in the these races will attract more customers to their ordinary production models. In the 1990 season, Japan showed 22 hours of sportscar racing on television. This was the year that the Sauber Mercedes Team won the World Championship. At the same time, the sales of Mercedes' passenger cars increased by 23%. Racing for such high stakes means competition is very fierce. The teams are always searching for new technology to give them the edge over their rivals.

In the Sportscar World Championship engines must have a maximum capacity of 3.5 litres. The races are 430 km (267 miles) in length, except for the 24-hour race at Le Mans.

This is the Sauber Mercedes. Versions of this car won the Sportscar World Championship in 1989 and 1990. It also won the famous French 24-hour Le Mans race in 1989.

Information about engine performance is transmitted during a race from the car to engineers in the pits.

The Sauber Mercedes was tested thoroughly in a wind tunnel, so all the sharp edges could be honed off the car to make it as streamlined as possible.

The body and the chassis of the car are made from carbon fibre reinforced plastic. This is extremely light and very rigid.

Different bonnets for different circuits

On racing circuits, airflow at speed can lift a car up and make it unstable. But car bodies are designed to give downthrust, so they stay firmly on the ground. Bonnet design is important. The successful Porsche 935 was designed with two different bonnets, one for slow track and one for fast track. This is because airflow acts differently at different speeds. On fast track, the 935 was given a lower more streamlined bonnet. The slow circuit bonnet provided downthrust at lower speeds than the fast circuit bonnet.

The Chaparall 2J sports racer of 1970 had a suction fan to "glue" it to the road around corners.

The ignition system and fuel injection are both electronic.

The roof of the car was tested with a weight of 8.5 tonnes (8.4 tons). There was only 2.6 mm (.1 in) movement. When the load was removed the roof returned to its original shape.

The car's design is very flat which gives it a low centre of gravity. The 12-cylinder engine is located as low as possible.

Porsche power

What is it like to sit behind the wheel of one of the world's most famous sportscars, the Porsche 911? First impressions are that the controls are all within easy reach. Starting is instant, the roar of the engine booming out of the back. Acceleration is fantastic and the car takes corners as if on rails. The suspension keeps the car flat on the ground and stable, but absorbs bumps well enough to give a firm, smooth ride. Top speed is 250 km/h (155 mph) and the faster it goes, the quieter it is. Truly this is a great sportscar!

In the World Championship, all sportscars that have raced 90% of the winner's distance are counted as finishers.

Grand Prix racing

Grand Prix racing cars are the kings of the track. Every year they compete for the Formula 1 World Championship and the cars have sleek streamlined bodies covered with bright advertising. Motor racing is an expensive business. Advertising sponsorship is vital to pay a racing team's huge expenses. If a team cannot afford the latest technology, then they will lose out to their rivals. Motor racing has three major categories. In the Formula 1, or Grand Prix, category cars have a maximum engine capacity of 3.5 litres. In Formula 3000 the maximum is 3 litres and in Formula 3 it is 2 litres.

In the cockpit, at the driver's fingertips, are an electronic turbo boost control switch, a multi-purpose visual display panel giving information about the state of the car's major components, a gear lever and rear light switch. GP drivers' racing suits are made out of a special fireproof material.

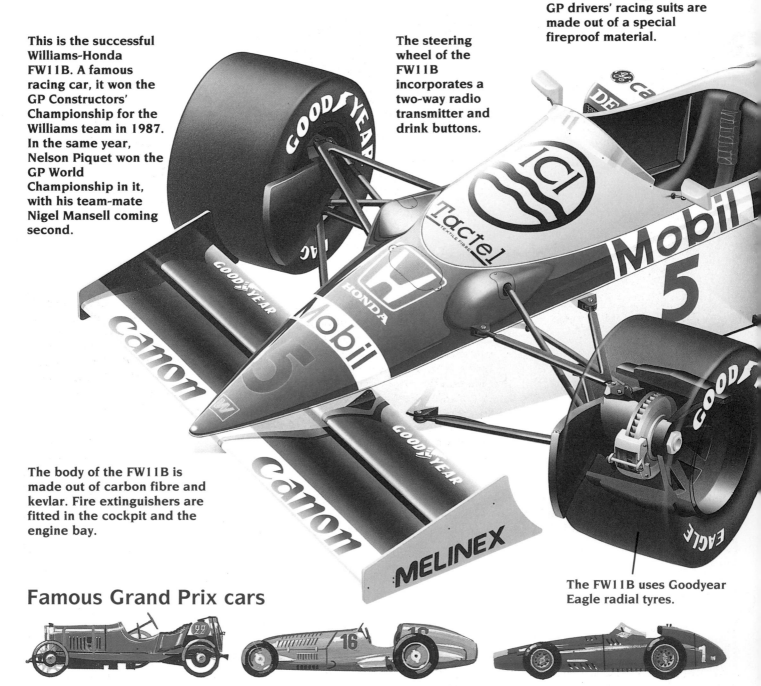

This is the successful Williams-Honda FW11B. A famous racing car, it won the GP Constructors' Championship for the Williams team in 1987. In the same year, Nelson Piquet won the GP World Championship in it, with his team-mate Nigel Mansell coming second.

The steering wheel of the FW11B incorporates a two-way radio transmitter and drink buttons.

The body of the FW11B is made out of carbon fibre and kevlar. Fire extinguishers are fitted in the cockpit and the engine bay.

The FW11B uses Goodyear Eagle radial tyres.

Famous Grand Prix cars

This handsome French Peugeot was one of the earliest racing cars, competing in 1912. Although its engine was very small, the car raced successfully against 14-litre Fiats.

The 1937 Mercedes-Benz W125, shown above, was the most powerful Grand Prix racer ever. Another successful car was the W196 which won 9 of the 12 GPs it entered.

This Maserati was an outstanding Grand Prix car of the 1950s. It was raced by two world famous drivers, the Briton Stirling Moss and the Argentinean Juan-Manuel Fangio.

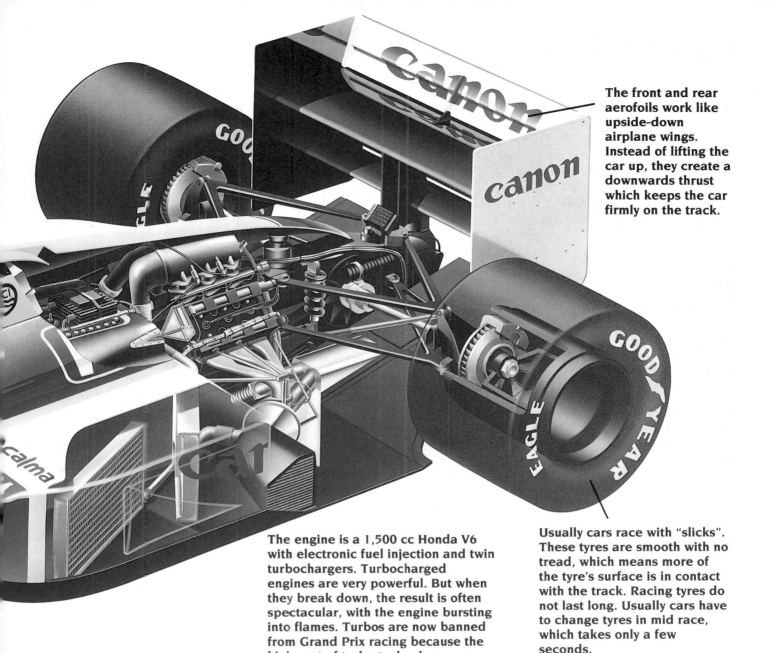

The front and rear aerofoils work like upside-down airplane wings. Instead of lifting the car up, they create a downwards thrust which keeps the car firmly on the track.

The engine is a 1,500 cc Honda V6 with electronic fuel injection and twin turbochargers. Turbocharged engines are very powerful. But when they break down, the result is often spectacular, with the engine bursting into flames. Turbos are now banned from Grand Prix racing because the high cost of turbo technology gave wealthy teams an unfair advantage.

Usually cars race with "slicks". These tyres are smooth with no tread, which means more of the tyre's surface is in contact with the track. Racing tyres do not last long. Usually cars have to change tyres in mid race, which takes only a few seconds.

Aerofoils

All Grand Prix cars are fitted with wings, called aerofoils to prevent them from lifting off the track at high speeds. Airflow around the aerofoils

creates downthrust, pressing the car downwards. This experiment shows what happens to a car's roadholding when wings are added.

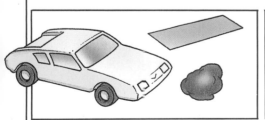

You will need a lump of plasticine or play dough and a model car, preferably made out of metal. Cut out a rectangular aerofoil 5 x 2.5 cm (2 x 1 in) from a piece of plastic, such as an empty detergent bottle.

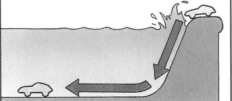

You can use water to imitate the high-speed airflow on a race track. The principle is the same. Fill up a bath and send the model car whizzing down the sloping end. The car should slide along the bottom of the bath smoothly.

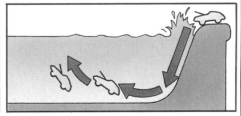

Dry the bonnet and fix the aerofoil on with the plasticine or play dough, angling it up as shown above. Watch how the aerofoil lifts the car up at the bottom of the bath. Now angle the aerofoil down and see how the car stays firmly on the bottom.

Bruce McLaren, from New Zealand, was the youngest ever driver to win a world championship race. He was 22.

Learning to race

What is it like to drive round a Grand Prix racing circuit? To find out, we visited the Brands Hatch International Circuit, which runs a racing school.

Brands Hatch has several types of cars for would-be drivers. After training in a Ford Escort, we took to the circuit in a single-seater Formula First racing car (see the section below, Training to race). It was a real thrill to experience the twists and turns of the circuit, and the blue and white track markings became a blur as the racing car reached speeds of more than 161 km/h (100 mph). It was important to keep an eye on the red needle of the rev counter to make sure the engine was not over-revving. The car's tyres screamed as we rounded a bend and then accelerated out of it down the straight. If tyres get too hot under the strain of fast cornering, they lose their grip. An experienced driver eases off a little to allow them to cool down.

Motor racing is dangerous and the driving methods shown here are for a racing circuit only, not for public roads. Also, speed alone never wins a race. Skill, responsibility and safe driving are all required too. The diagram to the right shows the Brands Hatch circuit. The red line shows the fastest way to get round, and you can see the clipping points for each bend and the gears a driver will use.

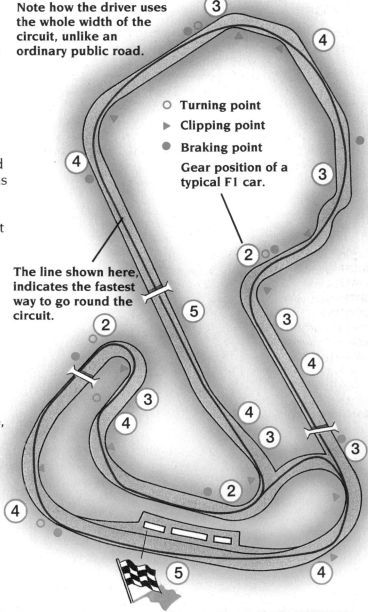

Note how the driver uses the whole width of the circuit, unlike an ordinary public road.

- ○ Turning point
- ▶ Clipping point
- ● Braking point
- Gear position of a typical F1 car.

The line shown here, indicates the fastest way to go round the circuit.

Andy Rouse, British Touring Sportscar (Class A) Champion, driving his Ford Sierra RS 500 at Brands Hatch.

Training to race

Before their first outing on the Brands Hatch circuit, pupils receive instruction from professional racing drivers. Then they undergo training in Ford Escort saloons, learning the importance of braking in a straight line and clipping bends.

Next, pupils progress to a Formula First single-seater racing car, which is capable of more than 193 km/h (120 mph). It is vital to keep the car on the circuit under high cornering forces and to make sure the engine is not over-revved.

Safety is very important. Full-face crash helmets and full-harness seat belts are always worn. After much practice, pupils are set lap times to beat, so they become faster and faster until they are eventually ready for their first race.

Juan-Manuel Fangio won 24 of the 51 F1 Championship races he entered.

Learning early

Road safety is vital It is very important that young drivers are well-trained in controlling a car wisely and responsibly. Brands Hatch runs a scheme for pupils who are under the legal age limit to drive on public roads. In fact, there is no age limit at all for the scheme, you just have to be over 1.47 m (4 ft 10 in) – so you can see over the steering wheel and press the pedals at the same time! Pupils learn basic car control, how to cope with traffic lights and junctions, three point turns and hill starts. ▶

Points of a bend

To the right, you can see the three points that a driver must learn when taking bends on a racing circuit. To keep up the maximum safe speed, a good driver must know exactly when to brake, where to start turning and where to clip the bend. At the approach to the bend, the driver must brake when the car is still in a straight line. Then comes the turning point and after that he clips the bend. If he fails to clip the bend and goes wide, he may be overtaken on the inside by a car behind.

Turning point

Braking point - car should brake in a straight line.

Clipping point at the apex of the bend.

Sliding

Front wheels "opposite locked" to steer the car through the bend.

Car brakes in this section.

As the car passes the turning point, the driver flicks the steering into the bend, pressing hard on the accelerator. This spins the back wheels, bringing the back of the car round. Then he turns the steering wheel the other way to keep the car on course. At top racing speeds, drivers can sometimes spin off the circuit when turning bends. There are many safety measures to prevent serious accidents, such as large bales of straw on either side of the circuit to absorb the impact of an out-of-control car.

Drifting

In a drift, all four wheels are sliding at an angle to the direction of travel. The front wheels are turned sharply into the bend. A well-controlled drift will result in the car passing the clipping point at the correct angle to accelerate down the next straight.

Study these three diagrams carefully, and the next time you watch racing on the television, see which drivers are the most skilled at turning bends. Notice how important bends are when a driver behind wants to overtake the car in front.

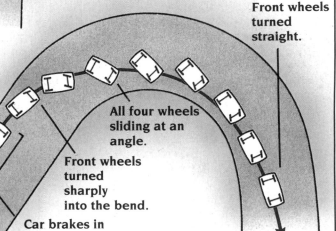

Front wheels turned straight.

All four wheels sliding at an angle.

Front wheels turned sharply into the bend.

Car brakes in this section.

At the race track

Grand Prix racing must be the noisiest sport in the world. The cars speed round the circuit with an ear-shattering scream. Apart from the noise, and of course the excitement of the race itself, the other remarkable thing about meetings nowadays is the super technology involved. Computers, electronics and even satellites all play an important part in a racing team's success.

Before the start, the cars will have raced against the clock. The car recording the fastest lap around the circuit is given "pole" position. That is, it will be in front of the others at the start.

This is just before the race starts. Race tactics will have been decided and the correct tyres chosen for the track and weather conditions. The driver is listening to last minute instructions from his support team.

During the race, a member of the support team will be in constant radio contact with the driver. The driver can communicate any problems and the team can advise him and let him know how the other competitors are doing.

Inside the team's control room, there is a massive computer. Important parts of the car, such as the fuel injection system or the brakes, transmit signals to a satellite. This satellite then relays information to the computer.

Cars make pit stops to refuel and have a tyre change only taking a few seconds. They also pull into the pits if they have mechanical trouble. The team will already know what the problem is from their computer.

Spectators at a race meeting often keep lap charts. These help you keep track of the drivers' positions. The drivers' names and numbers are entered on the left-hand side. After each lap, the car positions should be noted and recorded on the chart.

LAP CHART					
Nº	DRIVER	LAPS 1	2	3	
11	J. SMITH	6	6	6	6
20	N. HAUTA	20	20	20	10
10	J. SHUNT	11	11	10	20
28	E. FILLIE	10	10	28	28
6	M.				

Pit board

Although in radio contact with the driver, the team still hold up pit boards to show him his position.

Top row: he is lying seventh.

Middle row: 23 seconds ahead of the eighth man.

Bottom row: 9 seconds behind sixth man.

Control flags

At race meetings, another way of communicating with drivers is by waving different flags.

The flag of the country where the race is held ▶ starts off the race.

 Held still, this flag means danger. Waved - more ◀ danger, prepare to stop.

Warns of a slippery surface. This is usually oil ▶ or petrol.

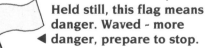 This flag is vital after an accident, as it tells drivers ◀ to stop instantly.

Indicates the danger that has occurred on the track ◀ is now clear.

Held still, car close behind. Waved, car closing ▶ fast or about to overtake.

 This flag warns that ambulance or rescue ◀ vehicles are on the track.

 A driver must stop at the pits when this flag is ▶ waved with his number.

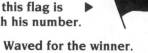 Waved for the winner. Held still to indicate race ◀ is now over.

Rally cars

Rally driving is a race against the clock and a test of endurance. Each car has a driver and a navigator. There is a set route which the teams have to follow and a number of check points along the way that they must call in at.

Competing in a world championship rally is not a simple task. Rally drivers have large back-up teams as there is much to do and organise. The team will have chase cars following the rally cars during a race,

service vans and tyre vans. Often there will be a team aeroplane spotting problems that may lay ahead, such as traffic snarl-ups

The rally car on this page is the Citroën ZX that won the gruelling Paris-Dakar Rally in 1991. The Paris-Dakar Rally covers 8,047 km (5,000 miles), much of which is across broken track and sand dunes in the Sahara Desert.

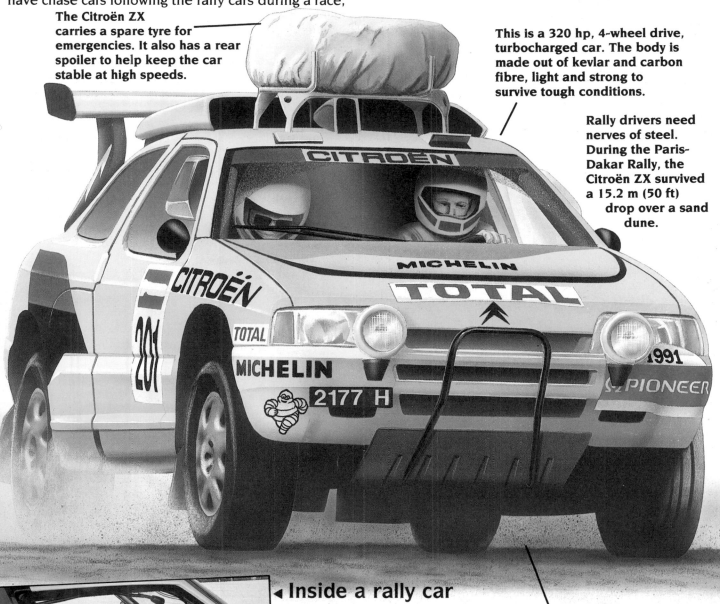

The Citroën ZX carries a spare tyre for emergencies. It also has a rear spoiler to help keep the car stable at high speeds.

This is a 320 hp, 4-wheel drive, turbocharged car. The body is made out of kevlar and carbon fibre, light and strong to survive tough conditions.

Rally drivers need nerves of steel. During the Paris-Dakar Rally, the Citroën ZX survived a 15.2 m (50 ft) drop over a sand dune.

◄ Inside a rally car

Here we get a look inside the cockpit of a Lancia Integrale rally car. A display above the heater controls can show information, such as speed, oil pressure and oil and water temperature. A Halda rally computer is triggered by a foot switch to the right of the navigator's footrest. This calculates speed and times.

The Citroën ZX is also an ordinary production car. Travelling at speeds of 161 km/h (100 mph) in rough conditions, the rally version needed many modifications, such as improved suspension, special tyres and a roll cage to give extra protection in an accident.

The Lancia Delta S4 rally car was so powerful that ordinary drivers could not control it.

Dragsters

Dragsters are fast and furious. They compete against each other in drag races and are some of the most colourful and eccentric vehicles you will ever see. This is a typical mid-engined dragster. The machine is equipped with aerofoils front and back, and a strong metal frame.

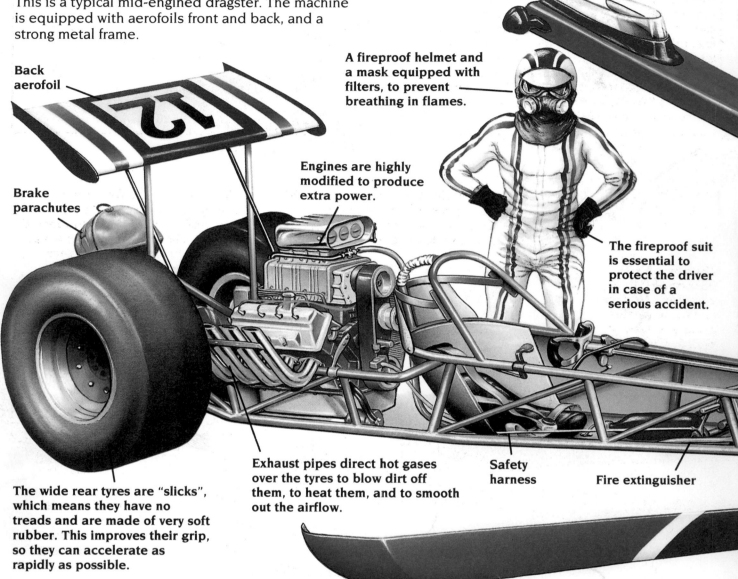

Back aerofoil

Brake parachutes

A fireproof helmet and a mask equipped with filters, to prevent breathing in flames.

Engines are highly modified to produce extra power.

The fireproof suit is essential to protect the driver in case of a serious accident.

The wide rear tyres are "slicks", which means they have no treads and are made of very soft rubber. This improves their grip, so they can accelerate as rapidly as possible.

Exhaust pipes direct hot gases over the tyres to blow dirt off them, to heat them, and to smooth out the airflow.

Safety harness

Fire extinguisher

The 5 second dash

Drag racing takes place all over the world. Dragsters race two at a time along a straight 400 m (¼ mile) drag strip. The kings of the strip, the AA fuel dragsters, look more like skeletons than cars. Any excess weight (panelling around the engine for example) is left off, and they burn a special fuel called nitro-methane to get maximum power from the engine. A fuel dragster's engine develops nearly twice the power of a "gasser", a gasolene (petrol) fueled car.

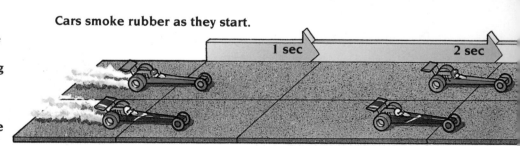

Cars smoke rubber as they start.

1 sec

2 sec

The "fire-up" road

This will give you an idea of what happens in a typical drag race.

The competing dragsters are push-started in the "fire-up" road. Then they make their burn-outs. For this, the drivers lock the front wheels and spin the back ones. The heat and friction of the spinning back wheels warms the slicks and lays down twin strips of tacky rubber on the track.

"Blond Bombshell" used an old rocket motor to push it up to a speed of 466.7 km/h (290mph).

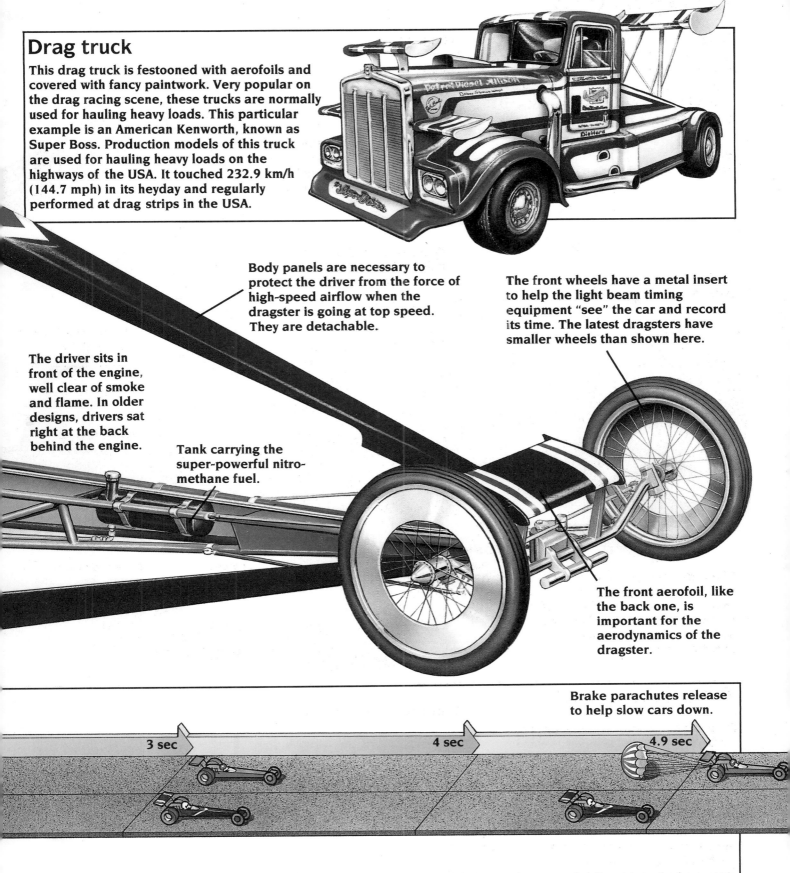

Drag truck

This drag truck is festooned with aerofoils and covered with fancy paintwork. Very popular on the drag racing scene, these trucks are normally used for hauling heavy loads. This particular example is an American Kenworth, known as Super Boss. Production models of this truck are used for hauling heavy loads on the highways of the USA. It touched 232.9 km/h (144.7 mph) in its heyday and regularly performed at drag strips in the USA.

Body panels are necessary to protect the driver from the force of high-speed airflow when the dragster is going at top speed. They are detachable.

The front wheels have a metal insert to help the light beam timing equipment "see" the car and record its time. The latest dragsters have smaller wheels than shown here.

The driver sits in front of the engine, well clear of smoke and flame. In older designs, drivers sat right at the back behind the engine.

Tank carrying the super-powerful nitro-methane fuel.

The front aerofoil, like the back one, is important for the aerodynamics of the dragster.

Brake parachutes release to help slow cars down.

3 sec   4 sec   4.9 sec

This improves the slicks' grip, ready for take-off.

The dragsters now move to the start line. A series of lamps, called a Christmas tree, flash a countdown sequence. The last lamp to flash is green and this is the signal to start. If the cars get off to a good start, they will manage a time of about 4.9 seconds. Average speed will be about 290 km/h (180 mph). Electronic equipment records the time and speed. As the finish line is crossed, parachutes are released to slow the cars down.

The "Eurosting" dragster used nearly 23 litres (5 gallons) of fuel for its 400 m (¼ mile) run.

Weird wheels

The extraordinary creations on these two pages have one thing in common - they are all amazing!

Since the beginning of motorcar history, engineers have come up with odd ideas, like the motorized pram invented in 1922, with a platform at the back for a nursemaid to ride on. Or the 1941 Le Dauphin tandem which could use petrol, electricity or pedal power to turn the wheels.

The Vultee Aérocar of 1947 was a car and an aeroplane all rolled into one and even had a set of detachable wings.

◄ The French Leyat Aérocar was built in 1923. It had a wooden propeller which pulled the car along at speeds up to 160 km/h (99 mph). It had two brake pedals, one for each front wheel.

Rear wheel steering

Wooden propeller

Single rear wheel

Rear mounted engine

Passenger seating

▲ The vehicle above is the Dymaxion three-wheeler of 1933. It was designed by the famous American architect Buckminster Fuller. The overhanging section at the front made the car unstable, and the rear wheel steering made the car difficult to drive.

Stabilizer fins

◄ These experimental American cars were Firebirds, made by General Motors in the 1950s and 1960s. They were powered by gas turbine aircraft engines. One of these models had a single lever replacing the accelerator pedal, brake pedal and steering wheel.

Fuel for a world on the move

Nowadays some cars can run on electricity and solar power, but the most common motorcar fuel is still made from crude oil. Formed millions of years ago from the decayed remains of tiny plants and animals, the world's oil reserves lie deep under the ground or seabed. The sequence of pictures to the right shows the journey crude oil takes, from the moment it is brought to the earth's surface through to some of its end products, like jet fuel and bitumen. Each grade of oil has its own specialized uses.

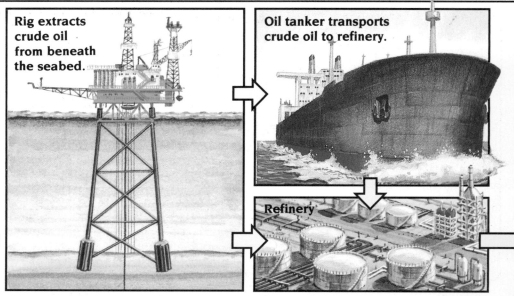

Rig extracts crude oil from beneath the seabed.

Oil tanker transports crude oil to refinery.

Refinery

The Panther-6 was designed as a unique and expensive car. The prototype shown here is a convertible two-seater. Production models had powered folding tops.

Aquaplaning and how to avoid it

At low speed on a wet road, a tyre's tread channels water out of the way, keeping it in contact with the road. At high speed, so much water can build up that not all of it is channelled away. The tyre then loses its grip and rides up on a film of water. This is called aquaplaning and can mean a total loss of control.

The Panther-6 had a six-wheel layout. The car's first set of front wheels swept the water to one side, so the second set could get a good grip.

This picture shows how the Panther's unique wheel layout allows safer driving in wet weather.

First set of front wheels aquaplaning, but still channelling water aside.

Second set of front wheels stay in road contact.

This "orange" bubble car was built as a publicity stunt to advertise a firm importing oranges. The shell was made of glass fibre, built up on the chassis of a British Leyland Mini. Several "oranges" were made and were fully roadworthy.

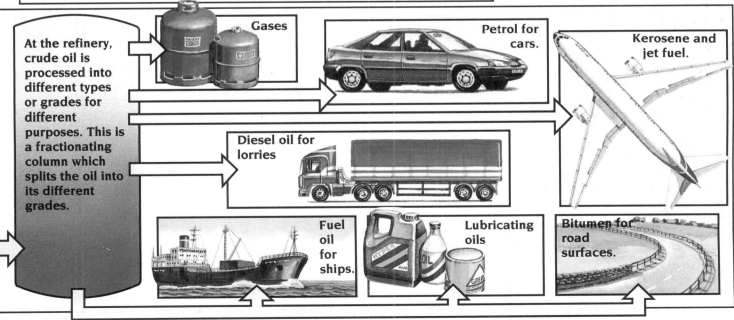

At the refinery, crude oil is processed into different types or grades for different purposes. This is a fractionating column which splits the oil into its different grades.

Gases

Petrol for cars.

Kerosene and jet fuel.

Diesel oil for lorries

Fuel oil for ships.

Lubricating oils

Bitumen for road surfaces.

A tyre rolling on a wet road at 80 km/h (50 mph) has to channel away over 5 litres (1.1 gallons) of water a second.

Car design

At international car shows, companies display their latest models together with special vehicles, called concept cars or prototypes. These cars are usually "one-off" experiments, testing different design and engineering ideas. Sometimes they go on to become production cars that are sold to the general public.

The Ghia Saguaro, shown on the right, was a concept car that appeared on the Ford stand at the Geneva International Motor Show. It was an experiment in designing a futuristic car for everyday use. It did not become a production car, but some of the ideas would have been included in other Ford models.

Big tyres, 531 mm (24¾ in) in diameter, for off-road as well as on-road driving.

The Ghia Saguaro

This concept car was developed in Ford's design studio at Turin in Italy. Here you can see the designers' pictures of their idea for the finished car. It had seating that could take from two to seven people and a large area at the back, like an estate car, when the back three seats were folded down. The back tailgate extended deep into the roof, to load very large objects.

Be your own car designer

The first rule when designing a car is to make sure that there is room inside for people. This means your first step must be to assemble the mannikin, shown on the right. Trace the body parts and transfer your tracings to a piece of cardboard. Cut out the shapes and assemble the mannikin as shown in the blue box. Now create cardboard car components in the same way and you will be ready to design your car. On the opposite page is a small sports car we designed.

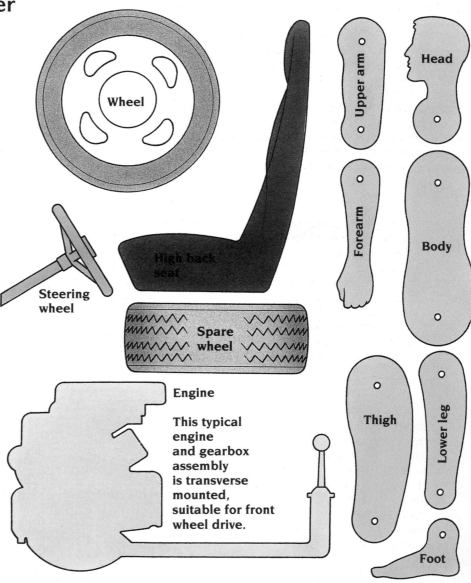

Wheel

Upper arm

Head

Forearm

Body

High back seat

Steering wheel

Spare wheel

Thigh

Lower leg

Engine

This typical engine and gearbox assembly is transverse mounted, suitable for front wheel drive.

Foot

How to assemble your mannikin

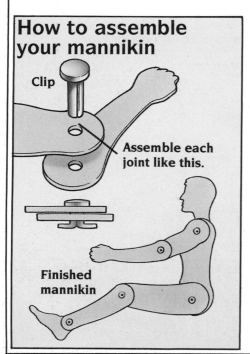

Clip

Assemble each joint like this.

Finished mannikin

The Morgan Plus 8 is designed to look like a 1930s car. But its speed is modern - at 190 km/h (118 mph).

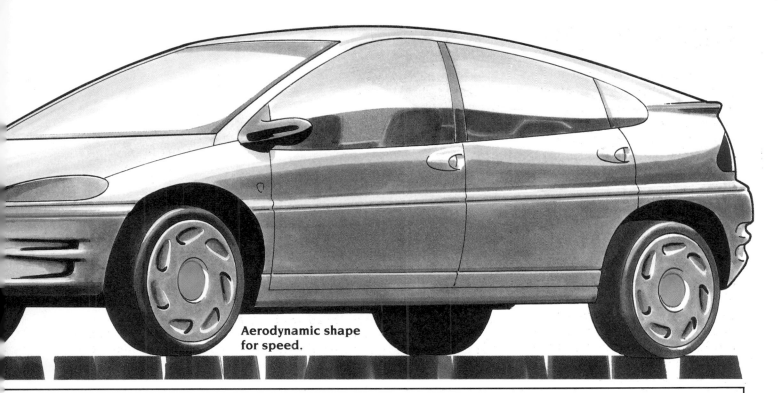

Aerodynamic shape
for speed.

Three steps to a sports design

First of all, decide what type of car you want to design. For our sports car, we decided on a front-wheel drive, front engine and four seats. The spare wheel was stowed at the front. Good streamlining was essential, to improve the car's top speed and fuel economy. The basic components were put in position together with the driver mannikin.

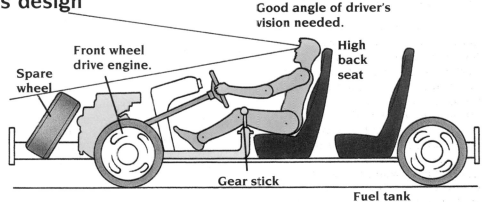

Good angle of driver's vision needed.

Front wheel drive engine.

High back seat

Spare wheel

Gear stick

Here the design has progressed a little, with the car body shape sketched in. We brought the seats forward to create a larger load space at the back. Then we moved the spare wheel to the back, so the nose could be lower and sleeker. The fuel tank was also placed at the back, in a lower position and protected by the crash bulkhead.

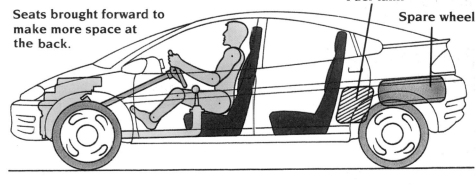

Seats brought forward to make more space at the back.

Fuel tank

Spare wheel

The final design has tinted windows and large front and back lights. The bumper strip all round gives good bodywork protection. The back door frame hides a tough roll-over cage to protect the driver and passengers in a crash. The tyres have a reflective coating, so the car is clearly seen from the side at night.

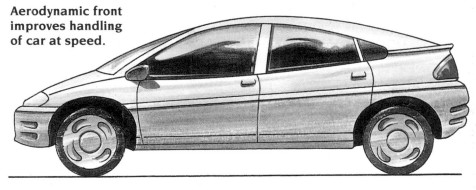

Aerodynamic front improves handling of car at speed.

The largest engine ever built for a road racing car was a 26.4 litre four-cylinder Dufaux of 1905.

Car production

A motorcar is made up of at least 15,000 different parts. To make these complicated machines quickly and efficiently, today's car factories are as modern and automated as possible. Usually cars are put together step-by-step on an assembly line. A conveyer belt moves lines of cars down the assembly line, so each worker or robot can add their part to each vehicle. Producing cars very quickly like this is called mass production. BMW in Germany use many robots for jobs that workers once did, like welding, drilling and painting. On these pages you can see car production in BMW factories.

1

More than 6,000 scientists and engineers work at the BMW Munich Research and Development Centre. This is where cars are designed and tested. Computers here are connected to computers in the factories.

2
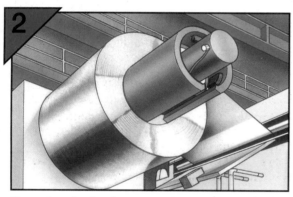

Parts for the body are made on the press lines. At the start of a press line is a roll of sheet metal. A section, called a "crude sheet" is cut from the roll. This then travels down a conveyer belt to be pressed into shape.

3
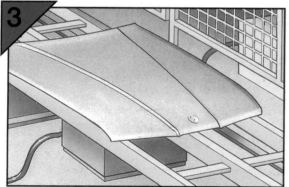

The pressed sheet, like a bonnet or hood, eventually moves on to the body production line. This is where different parts of the body are put together. There are 288 robots at the BMW Dingolfing factory doing this job.

4
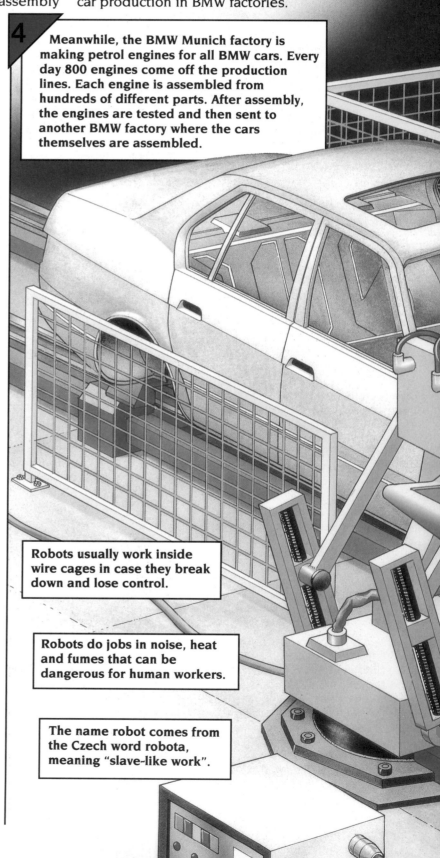

Meanwhile, the BMW Munich factory is making petrol engines for all BMW cars. Every day 800 engines come off the production lines. Each engine is assembled from hundreds of different parts. After assembly, the engines are tested and then sent to another BMW factory where the cars themselves are assembled.

Robots usually work inside wire cages in case they break down and lose control.

Robots do jobs in noise, heat and fumes that can be dangerous for human workers.

The name robot comes from the Czech word robota, meaning "slave-like work".

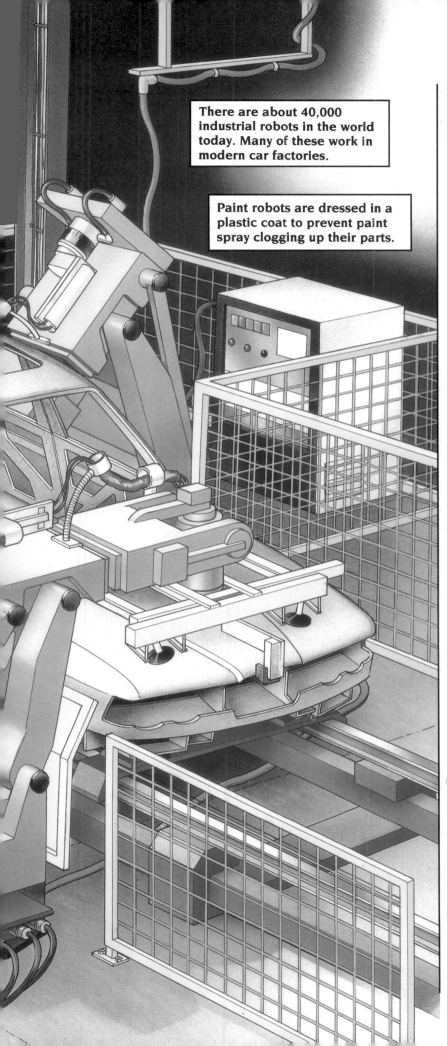

There are about 40,000 industrial robots in the world today. Many of these work in modern car factories.

Paint robots are dressed in a plastic coat to prevent paint spray clogging up their parts.

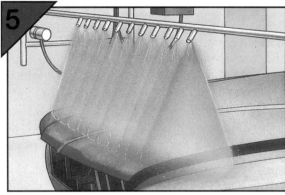

5

The body joins the paintwork line. Here it is cleaned before the primer is applied. Next it moves into the drying tunnel, where the primer is burnt on. Automatic spray guns and robots paint it and the last step is a drying oven.

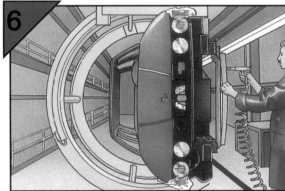

6

All the different parts of the car, such as engine, seats, windows and headlights, are added to the body on the assembly line. All these pieces are fed onto the assembly line by electric suspension tracks and hoists.

7

The entire production process from the pressing lines to a brand new vehicle is complete. Now the cars must be inspected. The electrical system is checked from top to bottom. The brakes and axles are thoroughly tested. The fuel and engine oil are added and waste gases coming from the exhaust are measured. Finally, the blue and white BMW logo is fixed to the hood and a layer of protective wax is added to the body.

Green cars

Petrol engines emit waste gases which can be very damaging to the environment, such as nitrogen oxide. This gas mixes with moisture in the air to become an acid. Clouds absorb the acid and when it rains, this acid rain kills trees and poisons rivers.

Exhaust car gases are not the only problem. Car production uses much energy and many raw materials. Recycling would protect the earth's resources. On these pages you will see how new technology is giving us a greener motorcar.

The Impact

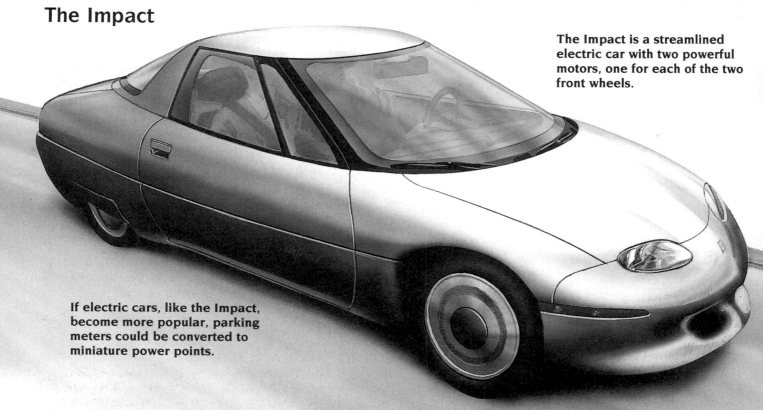

The Impact is a streamlined electric car with two powerful motors, one for each of the two front wheels.

If electric cars, like the Impact, become more popular, parking meters could be converted to miniature power points.

Electric cars are one way of avoiding the harmful gases given out by petrol-engined cars. Up until recently most electric cars were very slow and could only travel short distances before running out of energy.

General Motors have now produced a test car called the Impact. This electric car can accelerate like a sportscar from 0-100 km/h (0-62 mph) in eight seconds, and it has a top speed of 161 km/h (100 mph).

Electricity to recharge its batteries comes from a power station that may be burning fuel and creating pollution. This means that although the car itself is not producing harmful gases, the power station is. But electric cars can be recharged overnight, using only surplus energy. If most of the cars in New York were electric and the batteries were recharged overnight, the power stations would not have to burn more fuel.

Recycling

As raw materials, like wood, rubber and metals, get scarcer, recycling is vital. By the year 2000 about 2.8 million cars will have been scrapped in Germany alone. This is a terrible waste of raw materials. Car manufacturers are now doing their best to preserve resources and avoid the waste. BMW has a factory to break up old cars. The BMW 3 Series car, shown here, has many plastic components that can be broken down and made into parts for new cars.

This is a BMW Series 3 car, partly made of recyclable plastic.

Blue: made of recycled materials.

Green: made with the best recyclable plastic.

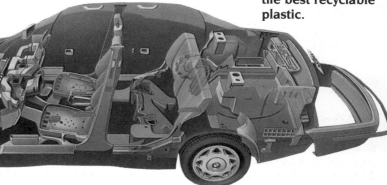

Cars emit carbon dioxide. Too much of this in the atmosphere traps heat making the earth too warm.

Catalytic converters

When scientists discovered that cars were causing a lot of dangerous pollution, they began to try and find a way of reducing the poisonous gases coming from car exhausts. Eventually they devised a simple piece of equipment fitted to the exhaust called a catalytic converter, which can get rid of most of the poisonous gases. This means that a car's pollution can be reduced by as much as 90%. In the USA, all new cars must have a catalytic converter.

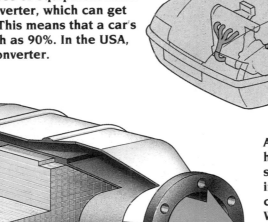

Position of catalytic converter.

Poisonous gases from the exhaust are changed by chemicals in the catalytic converter to become less harmful.

There are no moving parts in the catalytic converter and it needs no servicing.

A catalytic converter is like a honeycomb with a surface area the size of two soccer pitches. All this is inside a stainless steel box about 30 cm (1 ft) long and 23 cm (9 in) wide. Waste gases from the exhaust pass through the honeycomb structure, which causes chemical reactions that change most of the poisonous gases and make them harmless. The chemicals in catalytic converters are destroyed by lead, so all cars with this equipment must run on unleaded petrol.

Sunraycer

Cars in the future may use energy from the sun and not emit poisonous exhaust gases. The General Motors Sunraycer entered a race in Australia for cars powered by this solar energy. It ran by converting the sun's energy into electricity, with the help of a special magnet in the motor. Solar panels at the top of the car trapped the sun's energy. The car was a very odd shape. This was to make it as aerodynamic as possible. The race was run over 3,138 km (1,950 miles) from Darwin to Adelaide. First past the post was the Sunraycer.

The Sunraycer is completely pollution free.

The Sunraycer's shape was designed to be as streamlined as possible for low speeds.

Unleaded petrol

Lead is added to petrol because it helps engines run more smoothly. But it passes through the engine and out through the exhaust into the air that we breathe. Lead is a poison that can cause brain damage, so it is a dangerous pollutant. People living in cities are the most seriously affected, especially children. Nowadays governments all over the world are encouraging motorists to use unleaded petrol, that is petrol without the extra lead in it. Eventually all petrol should be unleaded. This will cut most of the lead pollution.

Every car produces nearly four times its own weight of the greenhouse gas, carbon dioxide, every year.

The world land speed record

In 1983, Richard Noble from Britain broke the world land speed record. This was the first time it had been broken for 13 years. His car, Thrust 2, travelled at an average speed of 1,019.63 km/h (633.60 mph). Richard beat the previous record set by the American Gary Gabelich in Blue Flame by just 18.01 km/h (11.19 mph). This new land speed record came after nine years of planning and hard work.

When competing for the world record, a car must make two runs over the same measured 1.6 km (1 mile). Both passes must be made within a period of 60 minutes. Speed is calculated from an average of the two runs. Cars gather speed before the starting post. This is called a flying start. The top speed Thrust 2 achieved was 1,047.46 km/h (650.89 mph).

Thrust 2 was a one-off vehicle built just to break the record. A Rolls-Royce Avon 302 engine was used from a Lightning fighter aircraft.

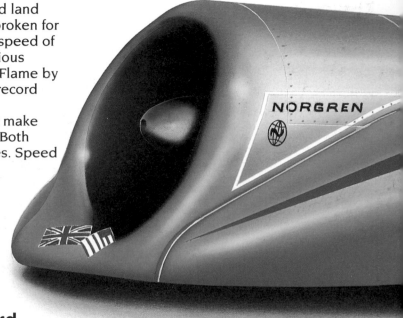

La Jamais Contente

In 1899, the bullet-shaped electric-powered La Jamais Contente (French for "The Never Satisfied") became the first car to travel over 100 km/h (62 mph). It must have been a very bumpy ride with those big wheels.
▼

Bluebird

Donald Campbell broke the world land speed record in 1964. He reached a speed of 645 km/h (401 mph) in his car Bluebird on the dry bed of Lake Eyre, in Australia. The car's power came from a gas turbine engine. Donald Campbell's father Malcolm also held the world land speed record and won the title many times during the 1920s and 1930s.
▼

Thrust 2 won the record on the mud flats of Black Rock Desert in Nevada, western USA.

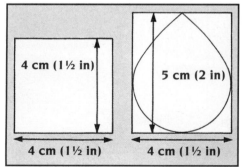
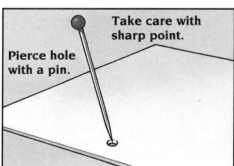

Streamlining for speed

4 cm (1½ in)

4 cm (1½ in)

5 cm (2 in)

4 cm (1½ in)

Streamlining is the science of creating smooth, sleek shapes that pass through water or air with the least drag or resistance. The less drag cars and boats have, the faster they go. This experiment shows how streamlining works.

Take care with sharp point.

Pierce hole with a pin.

Cut a piece of cardboard 4 x 4 cm (1½ x 1½ in). Cut another piece 4 cm x 5 cm (1½ x 2 in) and then cut it again to the shape shown in the first picture. Using a pin, pierce a hole in the centre of each shape, 1 cm (½ in) from what will be the front.

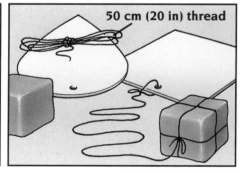

50 cm (20 in) thread

Cut two small cubes of plasticine about 1 cm (½ in) square to act as weights. They should both be exactly the same size to weigh the same. As shown above, tie the weights to the cardboard shapes with pieces of thread about 50 cm (20 in) long.

In 1966, Art Arfons crashed his car, Green Monster, at 967 km/h (601 mph). He survived.

Thrust 2

To reduce drag, the engine and all the other parts were wrapped up in a smooth aluminium skin. This streamlined body was important to give as little air resistance as possible.

Richard Noble sat in a safety cage to the right of the engine. Steel firewalls separated him from the engine and fuel tanks. The seat was made especially to fit him.

Rubber tyres can disintegrate at very high speeds. So solid aluminium wheels were used instead.

A right-hand foot pedal operated the accelerator, the HP cock (admitting fuel to the engine) and after-burner. The left-hand foot pedal operated the wheel brakes. The steering wheel had thumb buttons which released the drag parachutes. These helped the car slow down.

Blue Flame

◄ Gary Gabelich's Blue Flame, which won the world land speed record in 1970, was powered by a rocket motor like many other record holders. This meant power was not sent to the wheels, the car being propelled by the backward thrust of the rocket motor. This was mounted in the tail section and burned a mixture of hydrogen peroxide and liquid natural gas.

Fill up the kitchen sink with water, as high as it will go without overflowing. If you want to see the ripples your two cardboard shapes make, sprinkle tea leaves - or a fine powder, such as talcum, that floats - evenly on the surface of the water.

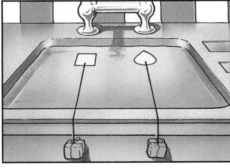

Carefully place the square shape and the streamlined tear-drop shape at the far end of the sink. The plasticine weights should dangle over the edge of the sink. It may help if a friend holds the weights while you position the shapes.

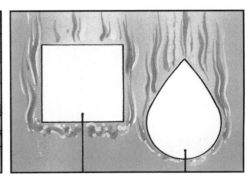

Now let go. Did your streamlined shape whizz past the square one? Its smooth lines give much less resistance to the water. Compare the turbulent ripples made by the square shape with the smoother ripples of the streamlined shape.

The White-Triplex record breaker of 1928 had three airplane engines, one in the front, two at the back.

Record breakers

Although the fastest car in the world now travels at 1,019 km/h (633 mph), it is by no means the fastest vehicle. Nowadays planes and rockets claim that record. Yet curiously enough, in 1906, for one year only, the fastest vehicle of all was a car. Called the Stanley Wogglebug, this steam-powered car set the record at 196 km/h (122 mph). It once reached 241 km/h (150 mph) before crashing on a beach. Speed records and championship races are big business now. The humble Wogglebug cost much less than the millions Ferrari or McLaren-Honda spend on their top-class Grand Prix racers.

The Grand Prix champions

Grand Prix racing has changed a great deal since Giuseppe Farina won the first GP World Championship in 1950. Crash helmets were not compulsory and protective clothing was unheard of. Later, names like Juan-Manuel Fangio, Jack Brabham, Niki Lauda and Ayrton Senna would claim their place in racing history by winning the Grand Prix crown. The cars they drove were to become more and more complex and safety as much as speed became a big consideration. Drivers wear flame-resistant suits and full-face crash helmets. Cars must be designed to resist the impact of a crash, and aerofoils are compulsory to keep cars firmly on the track at high speeds.

Year	Driver	Car
1950	Giuseppe Farina (Italy)	Alfa Romeo
1951	Juan-Manuel Fangio (Argentina)	Alfa Romeo
1952	Alberto Ascari (Italy)	Ferrari
1953	Alberto Ascari (Italy)	Ferrari
1954	Juan-Manuel Fangio (Argentina)	Maserati & Mercedes-Benz
1955	Juan-Manuel Fangio (Argentina)	Mercedes-Benz
1956	Juan-Manuel Fangio (Argentina)	Lancia-Ferrari
1957	Juan-Manuel Fangio (Argentina)	Maserati
1958	Mike Hawthorn (England)	Ferrari
1959	Jack Brabham (Australia)	Cooper-Climax
1960	Jack Brabham (Australia)	Cooper-Climax
1961	Phil Hill (USA)	Ferrari
1962	Graham Hill (England)	BRM
1963	Jim Clark (Scotland)	Lotus-Climax
1964	John Surtees (England)	Ferrari
1965	Jim Clark (Scotland)	Lotus-Climax
1966	Jack Brabham (Australia)	Brabham Repco
1967	Denny Hulme (New Zealand)	Brabham Repco
1968	Graham Hill (England)	Lotus-Ford
1969	Jackie Stewart (Scotland)	Matra-Ford
1970	Jochen Rindt (Austria)	Lotus-Ford
1971	Jackie Stewart (Scotland)	Tyrell-Ford
1972	Emerson Fittipaldi (Brazil)	Lotus-Ford
1973	Jackie Stewart (Scotland)	Tyrell-Ford
1974	Emerson Fittipaldi (Brazil)	McLaren-Ford
1975	Niki Lauda (Austria)	Ferrari
1976	James Hunt (England)	McLaren-Ford
1977	Niki Lauda (Austria)	Ferrari
1978	Mario Andretti (USA)	Lotus-Ford
1979	Jodi Scheckter (South Africa)	Ferrari
1980	Alan Jones (Australia)	Williams-Ford
1981	Nelson Piquet (Brazil)	Brabham-Ford
1982	Keke Rosburg (Finland)	Williams-Ford
1983	Nelson Piquet (Brazil)	Brabham-BMW
1984	Niki Lauda (Austria)	McLaren-Tag
1985	Alain Prost (France)	McLaren-Tag
1986	Alain Prost (France)	McLaren-Tag
1987	Nelson Piquet (Brazil)	Williams-Honda
1988	Ayrton Senna (Brazil)	McLaren-Honda
1989	Alain Prost (France)	McLaren-Honda
1990	Ayrton Senna (Brazil)	McLaren-Honda
1991	Ayrton Senna (Brazil)	McLaren-Honda

Champion tracks

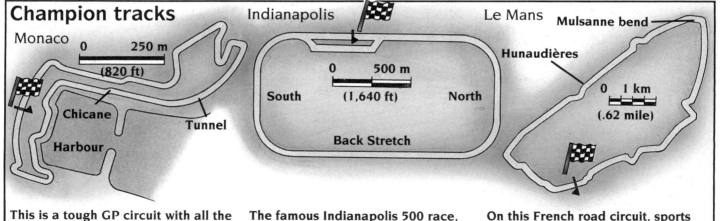

Monaco — 0 250 m (820 ft) — Chicane, Tunnel, Harbour

Indianapolis — 0 500 m (1,640 ft) — South, North, Back Stretch

Le Mans — Mulsanne bend, Hunaudières — 0 1 km (.62 mile)

This is a tough GP circuit with all the twists and turns in what are Monaco's public roads. Passing is difficult so the driver who starts at the head of the race has the best chance of winning.

The famous Indianapolis 500 race, over a distance of 805 km (500 miles) takes place on this American circuit. Unlike GP circuits, there are only four corners and two huge straight stretches.

On this French road circuit, sports cars, such as Mercedes-Benz and Porsche, compete in the famous 24-hour endurance race. The car which covers the greatest distance in the 24 hours wins the race.

Sir Jack Brabham won the GP World Championship twice as a driver and twice as a constructor.

Champion speeds

The world land speed record always attracts a lot of interest. In some years, several people tried to break the record, but only a few succeeded. The chart here lists the fastest record-holders and their speeds, at the end of each year in which the record was broken.

Sir Malcolm Campbell was a Briton who became famous for breaking the world land speed record and the world water speed record many times. His son Donald (see page 28) also raced cars and boats, aiming to be the fastest in the world.

All Malcolm Campbell's racing machines, for land and water, were given the name Bluebird after the play of the same name by Maurice Maeterlinck

Vertical axis scale: 0 — 200 km/h — 400 km/h — 600 km/h — 800 km/h — 1,000 km/h

Year	Driver	Speed
1898	G. de Chasseloup-Laubat	Jeantaud 63.15 km/h (39.24 mph)
1899	C. Jenatzy	Jenatzy 105.88 km/h (65.79 mph)
1902	M. Augières	Mors 122.00 km/h (75.81 mph)
1903	A. Duray	Gobron-Brillié 136.36 km/h (84.73 mph)
1904	P. Baras	Darracq 168.20 (104.52 mph)
1905	V. Hémery	Darracq 176.46 km/h (109.65 mph)
1906	F. Marriott	Stanley 195.64 km/h (121.57 mph)
1909	V. Hémery	Benz 202.69 km/h (125.95 mph)
1910	B. Oldfield	Benz 211.98 km/h (131.72 mph)
1922	K. Lee Guiness	Sunbeam 215.25 km/h (133.76 mph)
1924	M. Campbell	Sunbeam 235.22 km/h (146.17 mph)
1925	M. Campbell	Sunbeam 242.80 km/h (150.88 mph)
1926	J. Thomas	Thomas Special 275.23 km/h (171.03 mph)
1927	H. Segrave	Sunbeam 327.96 km/h (203.79 mph)
1928	R. Keech	White-Triplex 334.02 km/h (207.56 mph)
1929	H. Segrave	Irving-Napier 372.46 km/h (231.45 mph)
1931	M. Campbell	Napier-Campbell 396.04 km/h (246.10 mph)
1932	M. Campbell	Napier-Campbell 408.72 km/h (253.98 mph)
1933	M. Campbell	Campbell Special 438.48 km/h (272.47 mph)
1935	M. Campbell	Campbell Special 484.62 km/h (301.14 mph)
1937	G. Eyston	Thunderbolt 502.11 km/h (312.01 mph)
1938	G. Eyston	Thunderbolt 575.34 km/h (357.52 mph)
1939	J. Cobb	Railton 594.97 km/h (369.72 mph)
1947	J. Cobb	Railton 594.97 km/h (369.71 mph)
1964	A. Arfons	Green Monster 863.75 km/h (536.73 mph)
1965	C. Breedlove	Spirit of America Sonic 1 966.57 km/h (600.63 mph)
1970	G. Gabelich	Blue Flame 1,001.62 km/h (622.41 mph)
1983	R. Noble	Thrust 2 1,019.63 km/h (633.60 mph)

The youngest drivers to start in a GP were Pedro Rodriguez (1961) and Chris Amon (1963). They were both 19.

Index

AA fuel dragsters, 18
aerofoils, 13, 19
airflow, 10
Alfa Romeo Alfasud, 4
aquaplaning, 21
assembly line, 24, 25
axle, 7
Bentley, 6-7
Benz, Karl, 4-5
Blue Flame, 28, 29
Bluebird, 28, 29
BMW, 24, 25
body production line, 24
brakes, 6
Brands Hatch, 14-15
British Leyland Mini, 21
Bugatti Royale, 9
burn-outs, 18
Campbell, Donald, 28
Campbell, Malcolm, 28, 31
carbon fibre, 10, 12, 17
catalytic converters, 27
Chevrolet Corvette, 9
Citroën ZX, 17
computers, 16
concept cars, 22
control flags, 16
conveyer belt, 24
crankshaft, 5
crude sheet, 24
Cugnot, Nicholas, 4
cylinder, 5
de Knyff, René, 5
differential, 6, 7
drifting, 15
Duesenberg SJ, 8
Dymaxion three-wheeler, 20
electrics, 6
engines
    electric, 26
    petrol, 4, 5, 6, 7, 26
    solar energy, 27
    turbo, 13
environment, 26
Fangio, Juan-Manuel, 12

Farina, Giuseppe, 30
Ford
    Escort, 14
    Ghia Saguaro, 22
    Model T, 5
Formula 3000, 12
Formula 1, 12
Formula 3, 12
Formula First, 14
fractionating, 21
Fuller, Buckminster, 20
Gabelich, Gary, 28, 29
General Motors, 5
    Firebirds, 20
    Impact, 26
    Sunraycer, 27
Halda rally computer, 17
half-shafts, 7
Indianapolis, 30
Jaguar, 8
    E-Type, 9
    XK 120, 8
    XJ-S, 4
kevlar, 3, 12, 17
La Jamais Contente, 28
Lancia Integrale, 3, 17
lap charts, 16
Le Dauphin tandem, 20
Le Mans, 30
Leyat Aérocar, 20
Mansell, Nigel, 12
Maserati, 12
mass production, 24
Matra Bagheera, 4
Mercedes-Benz, 8
    Model S, 8
    Sauber, 10-11
    W125, 12
    W196, 12
Monaco, 30
Moss, Stirling, 12
motorized pram, 20
nitrogen oxide, 26
Noble, Richard, 28
oil, 20

orange bubble car, 21
paintwork line, 25
Panhard Levassor, 5
Panther-6, 21
parachutes, 18, 29
Peugot, 12
Piquet, Nelson, 12
piston, 5
pit boards, 16
pole position, 16
Porsche
    911, 4, 11
    935, 10
press lines, 24
propeller shaft, 6
prototypes, 22
recycling, 26
refinery, 21
Renault, 4
rig, 20
robots, 24-25
rod, 5
Rolls-Royce, 8
    Silver Ghost, 8
Sahara Desert, 17
satellites, 16
Sayer, Malcolm, 9
Skiff, 5
slicks, 18
sliding, 15
spoiler, 17
sportscars, 8, 9, 10-11, 26
Stanley Wogglebug, 30
steam carriages, 4
steering, 6
streamlining, 28-29
Super Boss, 19
suspension, 6
Thrust 2, 28
transmission, 6
Vultee Aérocar, 20
Williams-Honda FW11B, 12-13
wind tunnel, 10

Going further

There are many books and magazines about all aspects of cars and motoring. Some cover the history of motoring, others deal with Grand Prix racing, sportscars or classic cars. A few of the most useful are listed here.

Books

The Eyewitness Guide to Cars (Dorling Kindersley)
Car Talk Nigel Fryatt (Simon & Schuster Young Books)
The World's Fastest Cars Alex Gabbard & Graham Robson
   (Haynes)

Sporting Supercars Walton & Cadell (McDonald Illustrated)
The World's Fastest Cars Giles Chapman & John McGovern (Apple Press)
The Observer's Book of Cars (Penguin)

Magazines

Car
Performance Car
Grand Prix
Motor Sport
Autocar